P

Greece

Richard Spilsbury

WAYLAND

First published in 2011 by Wayland
Copyright Wayland 2011

Wayland
Hachette Children's Books
338 Euston Road
London NW1 3BH

Wayland Australia
Level 17/207 Kent Street,
Sydney, NSW 2000

Concept design: Jason Billin
Editor: Jennifer Sanderson
Designer: Amy Sparks
Picture Research: Amy Sparks, Jennifer Sanderson
Consultant: Elaine Jackson

Produced for Wayland by
White-Thomson Publishing Ltd

www.wtpub.co.uk
+44 (0)843 2087 460

British Library Cataloguing in Publication Data
Spilsbury, Richard, 1963-
Greece -- (Discover countries)
1. Greece -- Juvenile literature.
I. Title II. Series   949.5'076-dc22

ISBN: 978 07502 6447 1
Printed in Malaysia

Wayland is a division of Hachette Children's Books
an Hachette UK company
www.hachette.co.uk

All data in this book was researched in 2010
and has been collected from the latest sources available at that time.

Contents

Discovering Greece

The Greek mainland juts out into the Mediterranean Sea and is surrounded by thousands of islands. Greece is internationally renowned as a tourist destination, not only for its natural beauty, but also for its fascinating heritage.

A changing country

Athens has been the capital city of Greece since the peak of the ancient Greek Empire. It was the centre of civilization where theatre, literature and democratic politics developed. In the following centuries, the country changed massively. It was occupied by Ottoman Turks and achieved independence from the Ottoman Empire only in 1829.

Greece Statistics

Area: 131,957 sq km (50, 949 sq miles)

Capital city: Athens

Government type: Parliamentary Republic

Bordering countries: Albania, Bulgaria, Turkey, Macedonia

Currency: Euro €

Language: Greek 99% (official), other 1%

Greece is a European country that is about the same size as England. The country shares borders with Albania, Bulgaria, Turkey and Macedonia.

During World War II, hundreds of thousands of Greeks died when their country was occupied by German, Italian and Bulgarian forces. After the war, the economy collapsed and Greece suffered further during a brutal civil war, which left the country politically unstable. In 1967, a group of military officers seized power and soon ended the rule of the Greek royal family.

Modern Greece

In 1975, a new era began when Greece became a democratic republic. Political stability in the country allowed the economy to grow, especially under Prime Minister Andrea Papandreou, who was in power during much of the 1980s and again in the mid-1990s. Tourism and the shipping industry grew. In 1981, Greece joined the European Union (EU) and in 2001, it adopted the euro as its currency.

A country in crisis

Following the global economic crisis of 2008, and a period of borrowing money from banks, Greece could not repay its debts, which had risen to £260 billion (US$400 billion). European countries agreed to repay part of the debt if Greece reduced its spending. The government announced many austerity measures, which included cutting jobs and public services, raising taxes, and plans to sell some small Greek islands. The effects of the economic crisis will define Greece for years to come.

The Acropolis is one of Greece's most famous ancient buildings. In 2010 it was the site of public protests against the spending cuts made by the government in response to the economic crisis.

DID YOU KNOW?

The first Olympic Games took place in ancient Greece in about 776 BCE. During the Games, war with other states and empires was banned.

Landscape and climate

Greece's 2,000 or so islands make up one-fifth of its total area and the country has thousands of kilometres of coastline. Inland Greece is dominated by high mountains.

Geography

The large Pindus mountain range extends from north-west to south-east on the mainland and is often called 'the spine of Greece'. Mount Olympus is Greece's highest peak. Greece is situated in a region that has many fault lines and these can cause earthquakes and volcanoes. Some islands, such as Santorini, were formed from volcanoes that erupted in the past. Less than 20 per cent of the Greek landscape is lowland, with river valleys and basins created by lakes in the past. Only 170 of Greece's islands are inhabited, of which Crete is the largest.

Facts at a glance

Land area: 130, 647 sq km (50, 443 sq miles)

Highest point: 2,917m (9,570 ft) Mount Olympus

Coastline: 13, 676 km (8, 498 sq miles)

Longest river: Aliakmonos River 297km (185 miles)

▼ Santorini is made up of a large semicircular island next to several smaller ones. They are the remaining pieces of a giant volcano that erupted more than 3,000 years ago.

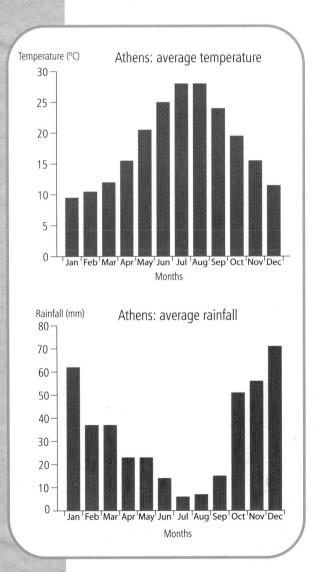

◀ Mount Olympus in northern Greece is made up of 52 rocky peaks with steep wooded slopes.

Climate

Greece has a typical Mediterranean climate. In summer, it is warm or hot across the country and there is little or no rain. In winter, it is generally mild, although there can be spells of very cold weather and it can snow, though this happens mostly in the mountain regions and rarely on the islands. Winter is the wettest season. Spring and autumn are short seasons when the weather can be very changeable. The amount of sunshine varies from four to five hours a day in midwinter to as many as 14 hours a day in midsummer.

Extreme heat

Sometimes, in inland Greece during the summer, there are heatwaves. During a heatwave, temperatures can reach above 100 °F (38 °C) for a day or more. Heatwaves can cause heatstroke, which may result in headaches, dizziness and even death. During a heatwave, people use a lot of power to run air-conditioning systems and this can cause power shortages. The intense heat and lack of rain can also cause widespread forest fires and water shortages.

Population and health

The Greek population is shrinking – one-fifth of Greeks are older than 65, and the birth rate is lower than the death rate. However, this may change in the future, depending on migration rates and the effectiveness of the healthcare system.

Population

Most of the population are ethnic Greeks but there are some smaller ethnic groups living in the country. These include Macedonians, Albanians and Turks, some of whose ancestors became Greek citizens following border disputes between Greece and its neighbouring countries. They also include Roma, commonly known as *Tsingani*, who move around the country during the year.

Migration

The biggest cause of migration in Greece is its economy. In the late nineteenth century, about one-sixth of the Greek population emigrated to the USA and Egypt when the price of currants, the major agricultural export, fell. After World War II, there was a second wave of economic emigration to countries, such as Germany and Australia.

▶ The ethnic mix in Greece is gradually changing through immigration. These African immigrants are selling goods on the streets of Athens.

Facts at a glance

Total population: 11.1 million

Life expectancy at birth: 80 years

Children dying before the age of five: 0.6%

Ethnic composition: Greek 93%, other (foreign citizens) 7%

Today 5 million Greeks live overseas, sometimes grouped in particular cities. For example, in Australia, Melbourne's Greek population is bigger than that in all but seven Greek cities. In recent decades, there has been immigration of different peoples into Greece, many from poorer neighbouring countries, such as Albania and Romania, but also from war-torn Afghanistan.

Health

Since 1983, the Greek National Health Service has provided free or low-cost healthcare for its tax-paying residents. However, as most hospitals and doctors' surgeries are concentrated in cities, access to healthcare in rural areas is more limited. The World Health Organization ranks the Greek healthcare system higher than that of the UK and USA. This is based on factors such as longer lifespans and lower infant mortality. Today, Greece has the highest obesity rate in Europe and this, along with reduced health spending owing to economic problems, will put pressure on the healthcare system.

DID YOU KNOW? Greece has a network of special SOS doctors who visit patients' homes to deal with health emergencies. SOS doctors are independent of hospitals and clinics but the government pays for the service.

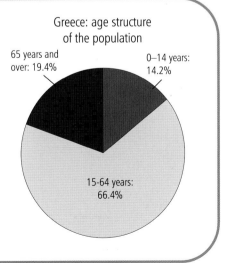

This woman from Xenia in Crete is 100 years old. Many people say that the traditional Greek diet of fresh vegetables, fish and olive oil, contributes to long lifespans.

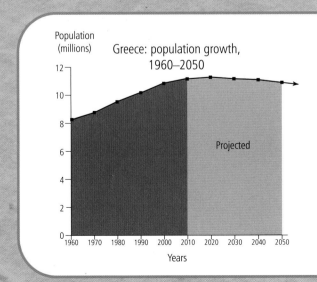

Greece: population growth, 1960–2050

Population (millions)

Projected

Years

Greece: age structure of the population

65 years and over: 19.4%

0–14 years: 14.2%

15-64 years: 66.4%

Settlements and living

Most Greeks live in apartments, rather than private houses. The apartment blocks are mostly in coastal cities where people can find work.

Homes

Most apartment blocks are several storeys high and were built in the first half of the twentieth century. At this time, cities expanded to accommodate the growing number of people moving from rural villages in order to find work. Today, homes are generally owned not rented, and a typical village home has room for one family. People living in cities may also keep village homes, especially on the coast, which their families use for holidays.

▼ Some of the most remarkable settlements in Greece are the monasteries that are perched high on steep mountains in Meteora, which means 'suspended in air'.

Facts at a glance

Urban population:
6.8 million

Rural population:
4.3 million

Population of largest city:
3.2 million (Athens)

DID YOU KNOW?
Ancient Greek houses were often built around open courtyards where people cooked and children played, and where women could spend time outside. Inside there were separate living areas for men and women.

Settlement patterns

In the past, the Greek population was more spread out and many people lived inland in villages, often isolated in the mountains. Today, two-thirds of the Greek population are concentrated in cities, and the capital, Athens, is the country's most populous city. Athens became important as an ancient trading centre between Greece and countries around the Aegean and Mediterranean seas. Many of the biggest cities in Greece, including Thessaloniki, are on the coast and have grown because they have good natural harbours for shipping.

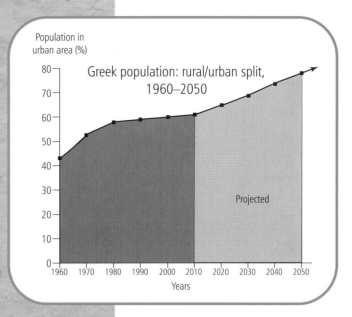

Population in urban area (%)

Greek population: rural/urban split, 1960–2050

Projected

Years

Illegal immigrants

Greece has the highest number of illegal immigrants in Europe. They concentrate near ports with the hope of finding work or travelling to Western European countries, such as Italy, to earn a better living. As a result of this migration, large slums have developed near the ports of Athens and Patras. Slums are a problem because they take over land, and put unplanned pressure on resources such as water and electricity. The Greek government has tried to reduce the slum problem and force people to return to their own countries by knocking down buildings and detaining the illegal immigrants in special camps.

◭ The conditions in this Patras slum were so poor that the Greek government moved the immigrants who lived there into military barracks. Immigrants choose Patras because ferries cross from the port to Italy.

Family life

Family life is important in Greece and families take care of each other. Different generations often work together, live near each other and spend a lot of time socializing together, too.

Greek family

In the past, men tended to go out to work and women stayed at home. Fathers were the dominant members of the household. This officially changed in 1983 with a Family Law Act that gave Greeks sexual equality. Today, many women go out to work, but in some homes the father is still the head of the family while the women do the majority of the cooking and housework. Most young adults continue to live with their parents until they marry, and elderly parents usually live with one of their adult children.

▶ Greek grandparents often have a close bond with their grandchildren because they live in shared family homes.

Facts at a glance

Average children per childbearing woman:
1.4 children

Average household size:
3.1 people

Marriage

Most people in Greece marry when they are in their late 20s to mid-30s. Wedding ceremonies are usually held in church and are followed by lavish meals, music and dancing. Instead of giving gifts, guests often pin or tape gifts of money to the bride's dress. Greece has a very low divorce rate compared to other countries in Europe. This is thought to be a result of the importance in Greek culture of families being close and spending time together.

Children

Today, most Greek couples have one or two children. As most Greeks are religious (see pages 14–15), their babies are baptized 40 days to a year after they are born. At this ceremony, babies are officially given a name, which is almost always a saint's name. Both parents are usually involved in bringing up their children and children also spend a lot of time with members of their extended family, including grandparents, aunts and uncles.

(see pages 14–15)

▶ A Greek Orthodox priest in Trikala baptizes a baby by anointing it with holy water and oils.

DID YOU KNOW? Since the film *Mamma Mia!* was filmed on Skopelos, tourist bookings went up 60 per cent. Many couples, inspired by the famous wedding scene, visit the island to get married.

Religion and beliefs

Greece is a religious country and almost all of its population (98 per cent) follow the Greek Orthodox faith. The Greek constitution guarantees its citizens freedom of religion, and there are other religious groups too, the second largest of which is Islam.

The Greek Orthodox Church

Orthodox Christians share many of the same beliefs as other Christians, but differ in the way they worship. A distinctive feature of the Orthodox churches is their grand services, which about a quarter of the population attend each week. Many more people go to the big annual services, such as saints' days. Greek Orthodox churches are full of religious icons, which worshippers honour with candles. Many people have icons in their homes, too.

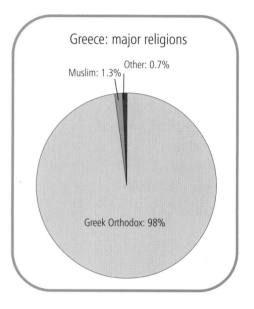

Greece: major religions

Muslim: 1.3% Other: 0.7%

Greek Orthodox: 98%

◀ Men train to become Greek Orthodox priests at special religious colleges called seminaries. Once they are part-way through training they may not marry. Women cannot become priests, but can live as nuns.

Church power in Greece

The Orthodox Church has a lot of influence on Greek society – for example, all children have to study religion at school and they pray together before starting lessons in the mornings. The Church also puts pressure on the government to take decisions that fit with its principles, such as banning gay marriages. The Church is also the country's largest and wealthiest landowner. It plans to build wind farms on some of its land to make renewable energy that it can sell to the country's electricity suppliers.

Festivals and celebrations

Most of the major festivals and celebrations in Greece are religious. Everyone celebrates Christmas. On Christmas Eve, families bake large, sweet loaves called *Christopsomo*, or 'Christ-bread'. Most people spend Easter in their native villages. As well as church services there are candlelit processions on Good Friday, fireworks at midnight on Saturday, and a feast of roast lamb on Easter Sunday. In Greece, people also have parties on their name day, the saint's day with whom they share their name.

▶ At Easter, the most sacred celebration in the Greek Orthodox faith, people set their tables with baskets of red eggs to symbolize the blood of Christ, when *He* died on the cross.

Education and learning

Education in ancient Greece was mostly for boys. It varied, depending on where people lived. For example, in Sparta, young boys were sent to military camps to learn survival and military skills, but in Athens boys usually learnt literacy, maths, wrestling and how to play the lyre.

Schools in Greece

Today, the Greek government provides free education for all children. School is compulsory from the age of 6 until 15. The subjects studied include history, maths, physical education, religion, geography, science and languages. After compulsory school, most young Greeks spend three years either at Eniaia Lykeia (EL) colleges, where they study subjects useful for university, or Technical Vocational Educational schools (TEEs) to study trades, from boat engineering to hotel management.

Facts at a glance

Children in primary school:
Male 100%, Female 99%
Children in secondary school:
Male 92%, Female 93%
Literacy rate (over 15 years):
96%

In ancient Greek times, girls in many parts of the country were not allowed to go to school and mostly learnt at home. Today, all young Greeks of both sexes go to school.

Language studies

The Greek language has existed since the fourteenth century BC. By the eighteenth century, it had more than 600,000 words, some from ancient Greek, and some added from other languages more recently, for example during Roman and Ottoman occupations. Then in the 1830s a new official version of Greek called *Katharevousa*, based on ancient Greek, was created. Although *Katharevousa* was taught in schools and used in books and newspapers, most Greeks spoke a simpler modern Greek, called Demotic, which finally became official in 1976. Today, Greek children speak Demotic but they also learn some ancient Greek during cultural studies. English is also learnt as it is important for jobs in tourism.

Greek Roma

Most Roma children living in Greece are poorly educated. This is because their families speak Romani at home so they get little support in learning Greek. They also change schools as their families move around, and they often get married very young and start to work without completing their schooling. The Greek government is trying to improve Roma education by training language support teachers and encouraging enrolment at schools.

DID YOU KNOW?
During wartime, Greek law states that men as young as 17 years old can be called to the army.

🔻 Just as Spartan boys were taught military skills, today the government requires all Greek men between the ages of 18 and 45 to spend at least 12 months in the army.

Employment and economy

Most Greeks work in the service industry, which includes government and private jobs. However, owing to its austerity measures (see page 5), unemployment is on the rise in Greece, especially amongst young people lacking work experience.

Jobs

The average wage in Greece is around two-thirds of the average across European countries that use the euro. Immigrants make up nearly one-fifth of the work force, mainly in agricultural and unskilled jobs.

Facts at a glance

Contributions to GDP:
agriculture: 3%
industry: 21%
services: 76%
Labour force:
agriculture: 12.4%
industry: 22.4%
services: 65.2%
Female labour force:
40% of total
Unemployment rate: 9.5%

▼ The construction of stadiums and other infrastructure projects ahead of the 2004 Olympics boosted the Greek economy but was financed by borrowing money from banks.

Many businesses are small and family-run so some people take several jobs, for example working in fishing and renting kayaks to tourists. Women make up less than half of the workforce, but this is a higher proportion than in the past.

Economy

In the early twentieth century, farming, herding, seafaring, fishing and traditional crafts were still at the heart of the Greek economy. The economy grew after World War II because of aid given by countries, such as Germany, to help repair damage and improve the infrastructure. It grew again after Greece started to use the euro because it could then borrow money more easily from banks. Today, 40 per cent of Greek gross domestic product (GDP) comes from public service jobs, including those in schools and government offices. Unlike many countries, the Greek economy also relies partly on payments from Greeks living overseas, for example in the USA or Australia, to family members in Greece.

Natural resources

One reason that manufacturing industries contribute little to the Greek economy is that the country has few natural resources. Greece has supplies of bauxite (the rock from which aluminium metal comes), stone including marble, some oil, and lignite. Lignite is a type of coal used in most of Greece's power stations, but it is more polluting to the atmosphere than other types of coal.

⏺ In summer, the arrival of tourists by ferry provides many Greek islanders with extra income, for example from renting rooms.

DID YOU KNOW?
Marble from Thassos, an island in the Aegean, is world-renowned for its bright white colour. It has been used since ancient times for building temples and monuments and for sculptures.

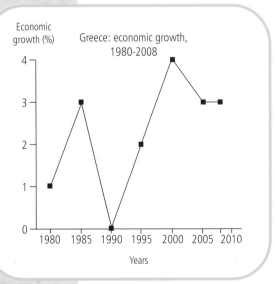

Economic growth (%)

Greece: economic growth, 1980-2008

Years

Industry and trade

Tourism and shipping are the biggest single industries in Greece, followed by manufacturing and construction. This explains why the value of imports into Greece is much smaller than that of exports.

Tourism and shipping

Today, Greece attracts more visitors each year than its own population, mostly from other parts of Europe but increasingly from growing economies further afield, including China. The tourism industry varies in scale, from sunglasses sellers and moped rental companies to hotel complexes and cruise ships. Overall, tourism contributes one-sixth of Greece's GDP and is found all over the country, particularly in Athens and the islands. However, the country faces competition from other Mediterranean destinations, including nearby Croatia and Turkey, which also attract holidaymakers.

DID YOU KNOW?
In the 1950s and 60s Greek shipping tycoons, including Stavros Niarchos and Aristotle Onassis, were some of the wealthiest men in the world.

▼ The World Heritage site of the Tholos Temple Sanctury in Delphi is one of Greece's most popular tourist attractions.

The Greek shipping industry has one of the largest non-military fleets in the world. Most ships are large bulk carriers carrying cargoes between developing countries and Europe.

Other industries

Manufacturing industry, or making things from raw materials, contributes about one-eighth of Greece's GDP. Factories are mostly located near Athens and make goods such as food and beverages, aluminium products, textiles, and chemicals. However, one of the world's largest cement factories is located at the port of Vólos, in northeast Greece, largely because the raw material limestone is quarried nearby. The construction industry builds not only public projects such as airports, but also private houses and hotels. During the economic crisis of 2008, the construction industry in Greece shrank and many people lost their jobs.

Trading

Around two-fifths of Greece's trade is with other EU members, especially Germany and Italy. It exports mostly food products, including grapes and nuts, dried fruit and olive oil. Other exports are clothing, machinery, and some refined fuels. Greece's major imports are vehicles, such as cars and lorries, chemicals, ship and boat engines, and crude oil.

⚪ Greek owners control one-fifth of all tankers in the world. The Greek shipping industry is thriving partly because of the demand for raw materials from growing Asian economies.

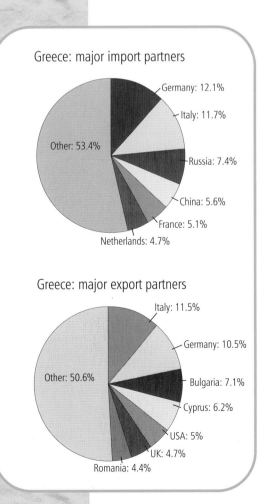

Greece: major import partners

Germany: 12.1%
Italy: 11.7%
Russia: 7.4%
China: 5.6%
France: 5.1%
Netherlands: 4.7%
Other: 53.4%

Greece: major export partners

Italy: 11.5%
Germany: 10.5%
Bulgaria: 7.1%
Cyprus: 6.2%
USA: 5%
UK: 4.7%
Romania: 4.4%
Other: 50.6%

Farming and food

Farming is a challenge in many parts of Greece, mainly because of the poor soils and lack of rain. Of the lowland areas in Greece, less than a third is used for growing crops; the rest is used for pasture, or left as scrub and forest.

Agriculture

On the plains of Greece, farmers are able to grow maize, wheat and cotton in huge fields. There are giant greenhouses growing crops, such as peppers and tomatoes, for export in winter. The country produces more black olives and high-quality olive oil than anywhere else in Europe.

Facts at a glance

Farmland:
36% of total land area

Main agricultural exports:
prepared fruit, olive oil, olives, tobacco

Main agricultural imports:
cheese, beef, alcoholic drinks, pork, wheat

Average daily calorie intake:
3,700

▼ Olive plantations are found across Greece, especially in the Kalamata region of the mainland. There are around 120 million olive trees in the country – that is about 12 for each Greek citizen.

Farmers also grow grapes, which are sold fresh or dried, or made into wine. Livestock farmers keep mainly sheep and goats as these animals graze on arid land, but they also raise cattle, chickens and pigs.

Fishing

Fishing has always been important to the Greek economy and diet. At sea, fishermen catch fish and seafood such as anchovies, sardines, mussels, tuna, octopus and lobster. There are also many fish farms around the coastline, and it is from these farms that fish is exported. Greece produces sea bass and sea bream.

Greek Food

The Greek diet was traditionally rich in fresh vegetables, fruit, olives and olive oil, bread, cheese, fish and other seafood, with meat a rare luxury. These foods still form the main part of the country's diet, but people also eat more meat and processed food today. Some typical Greek foods are taramasalata (smoked cod eggs), moussaka (a baked dish with aubergines and tomatoes), and baklava, a sweet pastry filled with chopped nuts and syrup or honey.

▲ Tavernas along the coast serve meals to tourists and locals. Fresh fish and seafood, such as the lobster shown here, are some of the most popular items on the menu.

DID YOU KNOW?
On average, Greek people eat around 25 kg (55 pounds) of cheese per person per year, which is more than any other nationality in the world. About half of this is feta, a white, salty cheese eaten with bread, in pastries and in salad.

Transport and communications

It was only in the latter part of the twentieth century that all Greece's villages had electricity and roads. It has been a challenge to provide transport and communications to the whole of the country because it has so many islands and mountains.

Water transport

Greek islands rely on regular ferry services to bring in goods and tourists. These ferries link not only mainland Greece with the islands, but also Greece with Italy. Inland, there are no navigable rivers. The Corinth Canal was built in the late 1800s to shorten trade routes from Italy to Athens. However, its shallow depth and narrow width mean many of today's modern ships cannot get through.

DID YOU KNOW?

On hilly islands with very steep, narrow roads, donkeys are still used for transporting goods from ports up to homes and businesses.

▼ Fast-moving hydrofoils, like this one, are a popular means of transport, particularly for people travelling between islands.

Air and rail

The main airport in Athens is linked to airports around the country, often near popular tourist destinations, such as Rhodes, but also close to major cities, including Alexandropoulos and Thessalonika. In the mid-twentieth century, the only airline providing flights within Greece was Olympic Airlines, which was run by the government until 2009. Today, there are several airlines offering internal flights. Although the Greek railway system is rather old, it is being updated. An important part of the improvement in transport links is the construction of the Athens metro, which is designed to reduce traffic congestion in this busy city.

⬥ In 2004, the Rion Antirion bridge was built to link the Peloponnese peninsula to mainland Greece and shorten road journey times across the country. At 2.25 km (1.4 miles) long it is the world's longest suspension bridge.

Communication

In Greece, around 5 million people use the Internet, which is less than half the population. There are around 2 million broadband connections in the country. Most Greeks find out news via radio or television, rather than on the Internet. A wide range of television and radio stations broadcast programmes across the country. The number of mobile telephones is high, with almost every individual in the country owning one.

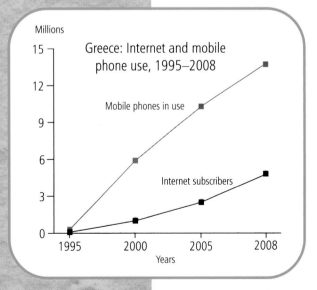

Millions

Greece: Internet and mobile phone use, 1995–2008

Mobile phones in use

Internet subscribers

Years

Leisure and tourism

When it is hot in summer, most Greeks spend their free time outdoors, socializing and eating, swimming or fishing. In small towns and villages, it is traditional for people to walk up and down the main street or shore in the evening, meeting and greeting friends. This is called the *volta*.

Leisure and sport

In the colder months, Greeks spend their leisure time at home watching television and gaming, going to the cinema or socializing in cafés. Playing sport is popular, too. The country's national and favourite sport is football, although basketball is also very popular. Other sports people enjoy include water polo, sailing, gymnastics and athletics. In mountain resorts, such as Pelion and Delphi, people also ski and hunt animals, such as wild boar.

⬇ The Greek basketball team (in white) was ranked fourth in the world in 2010. Basketball is a popular sport in schools and colleges, and many towns have outside courts.

Facts at a glance

Tourist arrivals

2000	10,130,000
2005	13,096,000
2006	14,765,000
2007	15,939,000

The arts

Greece has a rich arts heritage. It is famous for its ancient literature, including books such as Homer's *Odyssey*, plays such as Sophocles' *Oedipus*, and the sculptures and architecture that are still admired today. Traditional Greek instruments, such as the bouzouki (a stringed instrument), clarinets and lyres are still used to play a type of Greek music called *laika*. Today, laika musicians may also use modern instruments such as keyboards. Many Greek people listen to pop, rock and Western classical music.

Epidaurus Theatre was built in the fourth century BC and can seat 15,000 people. The acoustics are so good that everyone in the theatre can hear words spoken softly from the stage.

Tourism

There are several reasons why Greece is such a popular tourist destination. The country has World Heritage sites, such as Rhodes, Delphi, and the remarkable monasteries at Mount Athos. Tourists also come for the sunshine and clear seas to go diving, spearfishing, boating, and to take part in watersports. For example, the sheltered, wide bay and summer winds at Vassiliki make it a major windsurfing destination. Tourists enjoy visiting the islands to see their distinct cultures and features, such as the windmills of Crete. In addition there are festivals, in which Greek dramas are performed, as well as free concerts and open air films on offer in parks, for example in Athens.

DID YOU KNOW?
Tourism is so important that there is a special section of the police force, called the tourism police, whose officers are trained in foreign languages, to sort out tourists' problems.

Environment and wildlife

Greece has a variety of habitats, including forest, scrubland, mountain and coast. These habitats are home to a range of wildlife, including some which are endemic to Greece, such as the 600 types of wildflower that are found nowhere else in the world.

Greek biodiversity

Among the pine and chestnut trees of the northern mountain forests people see wildcats, boar, roe deer, and many birds, including vultures and eagles. Some of southern Europe's last remaining wolves and brown bears are found in the Pindos Mountains. In lowland meadows and scrubland there are many reptiles, including snakes, lizards and tortoises, as well as bigger animals such as wild goats and porcupines. Around the coasts there are 250 species of fish, squid and lobster, as well as bigger animals such as dolphins and sea turtles.

> ### Facts at a glance
>
> **Proportion of area protected:**
> 1.8%
> **Biodiversity (known species):**
> 5,522
> **Threatened species:** 27

▼ Rare Kri-kri goats are found in Crete's mountains.

Threats

Some of Greece's wild habitats are under threat, and this in turn endangers the animals and plants that live there. Trees are cut down to clear land for farming or building, and are destroyed in forest fires. Land is damaged by overgrazing and by tourism, for example when large hotels and other facilities are built on the coast. Fresh water supplies are also degraded by overuse, especially on islands, where water is used to fill swimming pools, for example. At sea, pollution from coastal resorts, shipping and overfishing are threatening many marine animals and plants, such as the Mediterranean monk seal, which is one of the world's most endangered sea mammals.

Protection

One-fifth of Greece's land is protected. This includes 17 national parks, including marine parks, two United Nations biosphere reserves and wetlands that are internationally important. There are also some specific projects aimed at particular habitats or animals. For example, the World Wide Fund for Nature is buying areas around the beaches of Laganas Bay, important nesting sites for the loggerhead turtle, to prevent coastal development for tourism.

◐ Conservation volunteers in Greece protect loggerhead turtles, for example by cleaning up nesting beaches and rescuing turtles injured when trapped in fishing nets.

DID YOU KNOW? The large Greek island of Crete is home to hundreds of endemic species, including many orchids, the Cretan spiny mouse, a shrew and a badger as well as the Kri-kri goat.

Glossary

austerity measures money-saving actions taken by governments to improve their economies

baptize ritual usually involving bathing in water to officially make someone a Christian

biosphere reserve unique region of land, water, air along with the organisms living and interacting there that are protected

civil war armed conflict between different groups within one nation

climate normal weather conditions of an area

constitution set of rules used by a government as a basic framework for their rule and laws

democratic where decisions are made by leaders elected by others

economy way that trade and money are controlled by a country

emigrate leave one country, usually where you were born, to live in another

endangered in danger of becoming extinct

endemic native and usually confined to a particular country or area

ethnic group part of a nation, race, or people with shared cultural traditions – for example, the Aboriginal people of Australia

export sell and transport goods to another country

extended family members of a family beyond the mother, father and their children

GDP gross domestic product, which means the total value of services and goods produced by a country in a year

Good Friday Christian religious day marking the death of Jesus Christ

hydrofoil type of boat

icon religious work of art, usually painted on a small wooden panel, important to Orthodox Christians

immigration moving to a new place in order to live there

import product or service brought from one country into another

independence free from the control or influence of other people, groups or nations

infant mortality proportion of babies born in a country or region that die before their first birthday

infrastructure essential structures, such as roads, hospitals, electricity supply and airports, for the people in a country or area

lyre type of hand-held harp with curved arms and up to 12 strings

monastery building or buildings where monks or nuns live and pray

monk a man who devotes his life to religious study and prayer, usually in a community of other monks separate from other people

nun a woman who is a member of a religious order

overfishing when so many fish of certain species are caught that the species cannot survive

overgrazing when there are so many livestock feeding in one place that the soil is damaged

republic government ruled by elected leaders, rather than by hereditary rulers such as kings or queens

saint holy person considered special by certain religions

sexual equality the equal treatment of men and women in society

Topic web

Use this topic web to explore Greek themes
in different areas of your curriculum.

ICT
Use the Internet to compare Greece's health data to that of other countries. Identify one data category suggesting Greece has a healthcare problem, and one that suggests the country can care well for its citizens' health.

Science
Greece is a country with 13,780 km of coastline and many tourists go to Greece to enjoy the beaches and coastal areas. Find out more about the environmental impact of coastal tourism, concentrating on freshwater resources and pollution.

Maths
The ancient Greek mathematicians Archimedes and Pythagoras are famous for solving mathematical problems. Find out what Archimedes' principle and Pythagoras' theorem are and how were they discovered.

Geography
Research different shipping routes from around the world. How do you think the Suez Canal in Egypt has been important for the growth of the Greek shipping industry?

Greece

History
Find out what you can about the origins of the Olympic Games in Greece. Why did they start, where did they happen, and what sports events were first included?

Design and Technology
Find a recipe for and create a traditional Greek salad. Make it look as attractive as you can and serve it with fresh bread. Evaluate the balance of ingredients in this meal – is this a healthy dish?

English
Many English words have Greek roots. Find as many English words as you can for these Greek word roots: hydro-, chrono-, phono-, photo-, poly-, philo-, arch-. Once you know the meanings of the roots, can you work out the meanings of the words?

Citizenship
Democracy is a Greek word that means government by the people for the people. What do you know about democracy in your local area? How do local councillors or mayors address local people's concerns?

Further information and index

Further reading

The Changing Face of Greece, Tamsin Osler (Wayland, 2005)
Welcome to my Country: Greece, N Frank and Y Hong Nam (Franklin Watts, 2005)
My Holiday in Greece, Susie Brooks (Wayland 2008)

Web

https://www.cia.gov/library/publications/the-world-factbook/geos/pk.html
Key statistics about the landscape, population, economy, government and more.
http://news.bbc.co.uk/1/hi/world/europe/country_profiles/1009249.stm
Country profile on Greece with key facts and links to other Greek websites.
http://www.guardian.co.uk/world/greece
Country profile plus all the latest news on Greece

Index